Convoluted, Memoried, Retrieved

Vivian Kearney

Convoluted, Memoried, Retrieved
Copyright
©2018, Vivian Kearney
Cover illustration © 2018, Vivian Kearney
Pukiyari Publishers

The total or partial reproduction of this book is prohibited. This book cannot be totally or partially reproduced, transmitted, copied or stored using any means or ways including graphic, electronics or mechanic without the consent and written authorization of the author, except in the case of small quotes used in articles and written comments about the book.

ISBN-10: 1-63065-095-1
ISBN-13: 978-1-63065-095-7

PUKIYARI PUBLISHERS
www.pukiyari.com

*Dedicated to Milo, dear soul mate,
our wonderful children, grandchildren,
families and to the family of man.*

TABLE OF CONTENTS

Convoluted 17

Convoluted Our Condition.................................. 19
Willful 20
Quest 21
Limits 22
Identifying With Nature 23
Wanderers 24
Each With Its Own... 25
Shadow Side... 26
Islands 27
When and Where.. 28
Blaise Pascal's Infinite Spaces............................ 29
For a While 30
Lit by the Kairos Sun 31
Somewhere in My Childhood 32
Open the Door.. 33
It Should Be;.. 34
It May Be 34
French Song – *La Vie Est Un Cactus*............... 35
One Small Step 36

Outside the Box, Inside Orbits 37
Societal Cleansing 38
Siblings 39
Shadow Chains 40
Once a Remark 41
What's Left? 43
Versus Determinism 44
Dream Smoke 45
But What About the Skin Cells? – Theseus' Boat 46

Network 47

After Marshall McLuhan 49
Family Secrets – Quoting Alan Bennett 50
February at the MARC (Medical and Research Center) 51
Psychologie à la Française 52
French Psychology 52
Yearning 53
Give Unto Caesar 54
Surprised by Music 55
Hallevai – May It Be 56
Mentsch or Cyborg 57
Weaving the Good Society 58
If We Worked for All That 59
Politics – Chess or Dance 60

- Purely Pragmatic 61
- Grass Roots Questions 62
- After <u>I and Thou</u> – by Martin Buber; <u>Isaiah </u>1:13-18 63

Torn **65**

- Any Planet B? 67
- Who Will Redeem 68
- Weeds, Grasses, Birds 69
- Entertaining Attack 70
- Sandy Hook 71
- Torn 72
- Metaphor Breaking Bad 73
- Sold 74
- Crocodiles 75
- Selling School Privatization 76
- A Year of Political Races 77
- On a Lovely Winter's Day 78
- Zero-Sum Game 80
- Down the River, Down the Street 81
- Begging the Question 82

Attitudes **83**

- Given on Thanksgiving 85
- After <u>Les Miserables</u> by Victor Hugo 86

Some People, Some Places, Sometimes 87
Crumbs Jump 88
Moved by a Visit 89
Recent Immigrant 90
After Mother Courage and Her Children by
Berthold Brecht 91
We Are Happy 92
That Room 94
Ageism 95
Prejudice 96
Once an Attitude in School 97
Clouds 98
Forgiveness 99
Beams and Splinters – Matthew 7:3-5; Luke
6:42,43 100
Better Opt for Optimism 101
Respect Them 102
Dear Sisters of a Certain Age 103
Empathy 104
Presently 105
Life's Banners 106

In Media 107

After Cave Paintings 109
Media Anomie 110

Classical Radio 111
NPR – We're All Ears 112
Paris Poet 113
Comparing Movie Endings 114
To Hold Your Hand 115
After <u>Nemesis</u> by Philip Roth 116
After <u>Lord of the Flies</u> by William Golding 117
PTSD – After <u>*Un Taxi Pour Tobrouk*</u> 118
After <u>Eugene Onegin</u> by Alexander Pushkin 120
Considering <u>Life of Pi</u> by Yann Martel 121
After the Movie <u>Trading Places</u> 122
After the Movie <u>*Canción de Cuna*</u> 124
After <u>*Un Coeur Simple*</u> by Gustave Flaubert 125
After Finishing <u>War and Peace</u> by Leo Tolstoy .. 126
<u>Mona Lisa</u> – Renaissance Muse 127
In the Internet – The Japanese Art of *Katzumi* ... 128
Shelf Neighbors 129
NPR Discussion of <u>*Don Quijote*</u> 130

Some People 131

Mindfulness Advice 133
I-Worlds 134
Absent From Class 135
Particular Conundrums 136
Christmas Party Memory 137

Just? Only? Merely? 139
Parental Prayers 140
Manic Depression 141
Whim or Necessity 142
Visit Again.. 143
Once When Subbing I Asked 144
Living in the Moment... 146
Annie and Dora... 147
Karate Novice 149
What It Takes 151
Thank you, Mrs. Smith... 152
Beginning of the School Year 153
One Special Day 154
Lessons at the Hospital... 155
Why Did She Have to Leave? 156

Memoried, Retrieved 157

Ever Receding 159
Keeping Memories 160
Retiring 161
With Daughter's Help... 162
With Son's Help 163
Lifelong Lessons 164
Sail On 165
Grand Central, New York..................................... 166

Together 167
Riddle 168
Gone Too Soon 169
Slippers 170
Once Also Received.. 171
Gratitude 172
Even More Beyond 173
By the Waters.. 174
Why Don't You Speak, Memory 175
Retrieved – Three Parables – <u>Luke </u>15: 3-32 176
Triangle of Forgiveness – <u>Luke </u>15: 11-32.......... 177
There Are Others... 178
Unwritten Diaries.. 179
Skies Over Lowlands 180
Southwest Celebration 181
At a Wedding 182
Marriage of Personalities 183
<u>After Thank God for Evolution</u> by Michael Dowd
.... 184
Devotions in Dance and Song............................... 185
Memoried Our Song 186

Convoluted

Convoluted Our Condition

Why are we so gray-natured, shadowed?
Where is our species going?
Who will mentor the mentors, lead the leaders
Give care to the caregivers
And instill more kindness, wisdom, goodness, grace
Into our spiral-laddered DNA?

Willful

With
Our thoughts careening
Like fireworks in the night sky

It's amazing
That we drive by
Others on the road
Mostly reliably

Considering
What willful cars
We all are
What intrinsic and extrinsic

GPS programs
Guide us

Over
What historic paths
Under what twinkling
Paradigm stars

Quest

Searching for identity
What might you find?

Relationships confusing
Beginnings mysterious
Feelings churning
Attitudes changeable
Health variable
Expectations contradictory
Goals tiring

And the cardinal of identity flies away
With the bluebird of happiness
While you are anxiously striving for
Understanding skies

Yet let the quest
Be for God
Who is love
And those much-pursued birds
Under a smiling rainbow
Return

Limits

Voice and range
Explorations and possibilities
Can be disguised guides
Good companions
For this ephemeral life
Up to a point

Yet needed are
Structures and boundaries
Of time, strengths, possessions
Places, responsibilities

Otherwise you would be floating
Who knows where or for how long
On oceans of possibilities

In your structured, limited boat
On those always uncharted
Future waters

Vivian Kearney

Identifying With Nature

Sun, our warming star
Moon, our cool, closer sphere
Trees, our praying companions
Rain, our therapeutic tears

You probably don't want us
To give you human qualities
Nor to yearn for your haunting nature
Before or after our human birth
Pleading for your identity-fleeing cures

We can't capture your secured songs
Though we share patterns of resonance
And we were all brought into existence
To be caring relatives and friends

Wanderers

We wander lost, wounded
On this earth, under the stars
Looking for lands not really ours
Pursuing happiness that cannot be caught
In the slip-sliding present

Reaching for the future which is virtual
Holding on to the past that cannot be hoarded
Even with selfies, pictures, objects
Journals, nostalgia

While echoing solastalgia
Yearns or mourns
For a time and place
That probably never was
Our former, faultless
Home

Each With Its Own

Time to think, talk
About all our stages, places

Each with its own peculiar
Opportunities, ministries
Joys, wonders, graces,
Pressures, sadnesses, worries

We're just chilling
In another age now

When those before
Seem warmer, greener
As well as rosier

By hindsight's glasses
Beautifully restored

Shadow Side

Each particular light
Is followed by its own shadow
And for different shadows
Specially sent lights

Vivian Kearney

Islands

We are islands
Bumping into each other
In a galactic sea

Whirling in time-space oceans
Carried by waves of history
And currents of psychology

O how happy when
Some present people
Offer to build bridges for us
Over troubled waters
To places of peace

O how sad when
One of those bridges crashes
Into the swirling, tigerish void

And we wonder
Where is the unorphaned
Milk and honey land

When and Where

The body
A tent, a fortress, a castle
For your soul

You don't know
Whether a slight break
A mosquito bite, a scratch, fever or chill
Will breach its walls

And the soul will
Float away

Vivian Kearney

Blaise Pascal's Infinite Spaces

The outer darkness
We so fear
Has stars

For a While

Considering
The proportion
Of our feet and legs
To our bodies
We are actually
Walking on stilts
Balancing
As fragile independents
For a while

Realizing
What could go wrong
With communications, expectations
We walk on eggshells
Balancing
Easily or uneasily
In some circles
For a while

Vivian Kearney

Lit by the Kairos Sun

Once upon a time
When I knew
Only of magical moons
And read about
Twilight-colored dresses
Suns and stars
Summers and falls
Were my banners

I dwelt in legends
And epical, mythical
Unmeasured lands
Of youthful leadings
Early learnings

That yet steer
Too countable years

Somewhere in My Childhood

The language of childhood
If I ever found out
What would it be like?

The joys of childhood
Sun-dappled through storms
Of some confusing homes

The toys and books of childhood
Foreshadowing fascinating forests
With cool trails blessed

The schools of childhood
Sequential ladders of education
Even in varied locations

The loves of childhood
Outstretched hands to walk with
Care to learn, remember and transmit

Open the Door

In the shadow of
The family castle
See the young being taught
Hear them start to talk
Witness their beginnings

Shown only certain rooms
Introduced to family dragons
Hearing acid words
Fettered and shaped
Into the dominant template
Mustn't let that die

Who will open
The ancestral door
To let those children
And their families
Out into a redeeming
Bright sunlight
Love-light

It Should Be; It May Be

Mothers who advised; mothers who didn't
Mothers who nurtured; mothers who couldn't
Mothers who rebelled and were haunted
Mothers who by war were cruelly hunted

Fathers who encouraged; fathers who wouldn't
Fathers who praised; fathers who didn't
Fathers who challenged quite stridently
Fathers who conducted lives rather strictly

Children who were acknowledged; children who weren't
Children who were cherished; children who were tolerated
O may all children be educated, protected lovingly
And may all families live long, healthily and happily

French Song – *La Vie Est Un Cactus*

We are
Some of us
Defended by

Cactus thorns
Against more hurts
Waiting for

Rains of compassion
That could turn
Spines into leaves

Able to
Collect more
Of heaven's rains

And sunshine

One Small Step

One small step
On the moon
Of unexpected grace

Far above
Our oft
Embittered planet

If multiplied

Could be
A giant step for mankind
To act on the basis
Of gratefulness –
Forgiveness

Vivian Kearney

Outside the Box, Inside Orbits

Outside our home box
There's another

Later a neighborhood
Plaid with lines
Of beautiful design

Mondrian knew it
And so do nested
Russian dolls winking

Then move further along

And you'll see
Gravity-led planets
Dancing a contained waltz

Or maybe a Texas Two-Step
Never out of celestial orbits

Societal Cleansing

Convinced to cleanse
Determined to decide
Who doesn't make the grade

Pushing to purify
You nullify
Others

And your own soul

Siblings

This one will repeat
One facet of
My original family's
Dynamic

That one will be
Encouraged, lionized

Another will be
Nagged and criticized

Yet another will be
Mocked and downsized

For every child
Has a different parent

Shadow Chains

It was a shadow
Line in the sand
Which in childhood
You were told
Not to cross

On peril
Of hurting and being hurt
Re-abandoned
Forgotten
And unforgiven

But it was a shadow
And nothing happened
Except the sound
Of shadow chains
Falling down

Don't pick them up now
O multi-yearning soul
Nostalgia for ancient fears
Will not make you whole

Once a Remark

Once a remark
Recollecting a memory
Is shared

About an often or once-met
Person, fellow traveler

A mutual
Relative, friend, acquaintance

About whom,
After all is said,
Little can be known
(For we are not God,
and most not even
Movie directors or novelists)

Can proceed to glisten
As an intriguing piece of mosaic
Apprized and often mulled

With which we try to construct
And review
Integrate
And reshape

Stories and portraits
For our own shrouded
Biographical
Castles

What's Left?

Surprise!
You're not your corner, your home
Not even your parents, family, toys

Amazing –
You're not your peers, games, appearance
You're not even your favorite teachers

Hard to believe…
You're not your job, your standing, studies, group
Not even your busy schedules, roles

Consider…
You're not your clothes, belongings
Not even your shelter, fortunes, surroundings

Guess what?
You're not your body, your senses
Not even your health or pains

 –What's left, dear God?

 – Your true name, love, will, voice, soul
That I your Father, Creator
Gave you, miraculously

To walk and talk with Me
To keep forever

Versus Determinism

For you are

Not a number – choosing predictably
To walk according to sociological
Mapped observation

For you are

An individual – none like you
With unique ways of traveling
Your own road

Prayerfully

With appointed angel
Guides to salvation

Dream Smoke

Alice, when you dream
Who are you, aside
From your known, your own
Real surroundings and awake
Identity?

If you smoke this
You'll never be quite sure

But What About the Skin Cells? – Theseus' Boat

Theseus floated in a boat bravely
Over the wide blue Aegian sea
Visiting, trading in many a port
Enjoying his fame happily

Until one day he worriedly thought
Better, more beautiful sails and wood
Would be apt for a hero who had fought
Notably, winning battles and loot

Seagulls also noisily criticized
– Get with it, Theseus, your craft is lame
So he rebuilt the lovely ship he prized
Plank by plank. But then he exclaimed

Every original part of my boat is gone
Every past inch replaced; nothing is the same
Then at what point did it change its identity?
It even behaves differently; should I change its name?

Besides, I gave the old materials to another
More frugal sailor, who made his own craft
Then is his boat mine and mine his? It's a real puzzler
But I'm always me, so no matter, Theseus laughed…

Network

After Marshall McLuhan

In this electric age
We wear all mankind
As our skin

Society talks in echoes
As we've been given
An eye for an ear
In this linear society

And where is
The seamless
Planetary village
Except in
The world-wide web

Family Secrets – Quoting Alan Bennett

Every family keeps a secret
Which is at least
That this family is not
Like any other

With its own
Unique druthers and bothers
Sent up to
The already noisy
Stratosphere / heavens

Dear Father
How do you hear
Each one?

Vivian Kearney

February at the MARC
(Medical and Research Center)

February on the calendar, in the air
Cardboard valentine posters
Smile from walls, counters
Family groups holding hands
Elderly guided in wheelchairs
Spelling love as cheerful, eternal care

Psychologie à la Française

Mélancholie à la mode
Ou joie de vivre en liberté
Laquelle est-ce qu'on choisit?

Pourquoi pas les deux
Quand-même
C'est la vie

French Psychology

Fashionable melancholy
Or irrepressible, free
Joie de vivre

Which will it be
Why not both?
After all
C'est la vie

Vivian Kearney

Yearning

Why do we want to live forever
If not to have forever, Lord, to love Thee,
Praise Thee, walk with Thee in heaven
And be with loved ones eternally

Give Unto Caesar

Discussing
The how, when
Where, what
Of science

Can keep you learning
Along those strings
Of nature's connectivities
For more and more
Predictability
Understanding molecules'
Proclivities
And creating
Useful technologies

But the why and the who
Questions of the spirit and heart
Do not belong
To pragmatic Caesar

Give that part
To God

Vivian Kearney

Surprised by Music

Some coins for a lilt of Haydn
For an echo of beauty, a smile

Fair enough pay to throw
Into a needy violin case?

Of a brother? A neighbor? A son?
Perhaps

For a two-way journey
Under the earth

Accompanied
By heavenly music

Hallevai – May It Be

When we don't bemoan
In long political speeches
Without positive issue

The glass ceiling
Or the racism
Or the incredible
Inequality

Having forgotten
Those previous
Painful issues

Then we won't even notice
That we've turned feminist, fair
And color-blind

And we'll all
Begin to be
True progressives
For each level
Of all societies

May we live
So long

Vivian Kearney

Mentsch or **Cyborg**

Haven't we always wanted to be cyborgs
Power-melding with surroundings
Even with our earliest weapons, transportation
Meddling with our limitations
By becoming something more

New age calls and most must respond
Proud to be citizens, not immigrants
Of technologies' cities paying internet dues
How pitying of persons still walking,
Talking without electronic cues

Shouldn't we also yearn
To be true *mentschen* besides
Helpful, of good character
Fulfilling kind missions responsibly
For a healthy, humane society

Weaving the Good Society

Communally, then
What can we do
To weave a fair society

Build a land, a village
Organize and support
A fair school system
Proficient transportation
Available health provisions

Construct a bridge
Back to Eden

Idealism, optimism
Can wash
Corruption, pollution,
Prejudice away

Love and kindness
Can sail over
Spiraling swamps

One day
One day
The dreamed of golden age
For everyone
Will be reborn

If We Worked for All That

If we had efficient
Healthcare for all
All over the planet
Always available
Public transportation
Free education to the
Highest level
And much lower
Economic inequality

Would we then visit
Each other's
Maybe disparate dwellings
Uncritically

And be unself-conscious
About sitting together
Hearing sermons
Talking about inclusivity
According to Jesus

Politics – Chess or Dance

Sometimes
Comes the image
Of a world-wide
Chess game

Pitting optimistic
Yearnings for justice
Equitable prosperity
Peace and a cared for
Nature

Against forces
Of destruction
Negativity, denigration
Selfishness

One step forward, two steps back
The dance isn't pretty

Purely Pragmatic

Expediently pragmatic
Is our narrow dogmatic
Way of doing things
Plucking visionary wings

Materialism longs to be
An overarching philosophy
But money isn't speech
Though it sure can preach

Grass Roots Questions

Does the pursuit of power have to involve
Circles of lies, unhealthy ties?
Can there be an altruistic leadership?
Can the one percent hear
The grass roots cries?

After <u>I and Thou</u> – by Martin Buber; <u>Isaiah</u> 1:13-18

Are those goals too low
Or is it too much to expect
That we feed the hungry
Remember they are neighbors
That we stop doing evil
And learn to do good

Isaiah, where and who were you
When you wrote this plea
From God's heart?

Torn

Any Planet B?

With this planet
We were given many Edens
Multiple lovely places
For paradise

But we ate the apples
Of industry, technology
Laced with capitalism

And exiled ourselves
By destroying the multiple
Fragile ecosystems of
This wondrous world

Will God grant us another?

Who Will Redeem

Are we like the careful Pharisees
Not picking wheat from Sabbath fields
Distracted by picayune red herrings
Ignoring dinosaurs of inequality?

Or are we like the casuistic Sadducees
Favoring strong Roman hegemony
Gambling their empire can bring peace?

Are we overcome already
By sadism's electricity
Abandoning genes of sympathy
Misled by chimeric flags of cruelty?

What cold, futuristic, purging fantasy
Looms on the horizon of sad reality
What child's innocent divinity
Will redeem us lovingly?

Vivian Kearney

Weeds, Grasses, Birds

Who are the weeds to be discouraged
Who are the grasses to be cultivated
Uniformly green, seen to be best
By neighbors similarly blessed

Why do we not only flock together
But also kill others of different feather
As if our race depends on others dying
As if God is on our judgment relying

Entertaining Attack

Fireworks, so noble, so pretty
Like a dream show on TV
We noted as we were rowing
Down the streams of our quiet lives

Yet some vibrations
Of strangers' real pain
Cries of tragic children
Tore through every now and then
Our veils of entertainment

Sandy Hook

Lord,
Give us back
Our more innocent souls
Horrified and shattered
By one who would
Open carry
And blindly tear
All our silken smooth
Warm and giving
Young hearts
Apart

Torn

Disparity despair
For those
Too poor for bread
Or healthy nutrition

While crumbs,
Cake or junk food
Are made available
Instead

Although others can
Eat golden meals

Changing their human hearts
To metal

Vivian Kearney

Metaphor Breaking Bad

Metaphor gone wrong
So wrong
Sees corporations as persons
Money as their speech
Buying, selling, legislating,
Tweeting, suing

But what kind of persons
Are these?

They have no souls
Nor sympathy for
Their customers, victims
Or nature

And what kind of speech
Is this?
A limited, bullying vocabulary

Guess who's our president now

Sold

In 2016 he had quite
    A romp
And his reign began
    With such pomp
His art of the deal
Made us all squeal
Until he sold us
    A swamp

By Daniel Anzak

Crocodiles

Hard to believe
That this values-proud nation
Has been led
Into banking swamps

And that people's needs
Don't really
Matter much
To crocodiles

Selling School Privatization

Are you hurting because we're withdrawing
All those helpful public school dollars
For our voucher-donated corporate establishments?
(We're trying here not to gloat)

Our private schools will only get better
As your facilities and offerings get worse
Who needs art, languages, writing, music
In this era of technologies' realities?

Our students are more motivated in what matters
Have less difficulties, are more serious
And if some are not, we'll just make sure
That these don't bother the others

By sending them back to you

How's that for a persuasive
Circular selling point?

Vivian Kearney

A Year of Political Races

A politician accused of
Going on seventy-four
(Aren't we all, he retorted)

Seriously declaimed
In a time of rigged games
Let's make things honest
And many applauded
And hoped with him

Will all be sensitized
Miraculously
And be made wise
In time?

On a Lovely Winter's Day

It was
A lovely
Sunny
Winter's day

Students contentedly
Quietly or noisily
Partially or fully
Answered their worksheets
About the beginnings
Of our democracies
And the long ago
Age of reason

While a man
Using the regal we
Was sworn into office
And said their public education system
Was for the birds

He and his cohorts
Were going to make it disappear
With some private passes (probably temporary)
Called school vouchers
Boasting the same plans
For an unaffordable health
Non-care system

Vivian Kearney

Replacing concerned policies
With good old-fashioned
Individual efforts
Sweat, worry and tears
And sickness

Much better, they said
For building up character
Than any interfering government help

And today was that sad
Winter's day

Zero-Sum Game

The materialist dream speaks sweetly
To each can be honor, wealth and glory
The lucky few should live with wealth and comfort
And be placed on pedestals by many neighbors

Someone has to win, why not me
Someone has to lose, why not you
Someone with my credentials should be hired
Someone who is different should be fired

Yet, why should we play the game at all
That may be the wrong dream that causes the fall
Of countless persons, many a nation
The reason the world groans for redemption

Vivian Kearney

Down the River, Down the Street

Sometime in our elementary
Class of school geography
We learned that old people
In frozen lands up north
Were cast off
In what must have been
A springtime melted river or sea

Now we can simply
Leave in an IV
And send the impoverished elderly
Person down the street
Where no one wants to
Open a good Samaritan inn

What would it take, Lord
To instill at all levels
Transcendental mercy?

Begging the Question

So many of us
About to fall without nets
Wonder at the few, the marvelously
Successful sky divers, travelers

Begging the question: Who are these beings
With golden parachutes and yachts of silver?

And why don't we
The not so fortunate
Decide to cooperate
Work for our common interests
And build together
Life-saving bridges

For everyone to cross over
To the promised land
Of happy living

Attitudes

Vivian Kearney

Given on Thanksgiving

Food!

A toothless old lady
Outside a chilly mini-mall
Was begging for something
This Thanksgiving evening

After we had eaten too much
We gave her a little money
For a hot meal

Not too fair a deal
In this food festival
Time of year

After <u>Les Miserables</u> by Victor Hugo

– Just look at this house, this palace, how nice
It has a sumptuous balcony
To look down on
The downtrodden
The homeless ones

– Just look at us under this overpass
We, the homeless ones, the miserable ones
Are reaching out to you, our fortunate brothers
For a hand up to participate equably
In your blessed, donating society

Vivian Kearney

Some People, Some Places, Sometimes

Orphaned weeds
Sprout singly
In cement gaps

Homeless pleader
Sits lonely
Under the overpass
And asks

For a handout
Maybe a dime
Or five dollars
For a McDonald's
Big Mac

Big city, huge country
Could make a little place
In its stone heart

Sometimes for orphaned
Nature and lives
To restart

Crumbs Jump

Crumbs jump and dust bunnies hop
Sweep one corner, another wants to be first
Housekeeping, cleaning never stops
And when is decluttering ever done?

Yet what Elysian fields have we here
In comparison to dirt floors, tattered tents
Where so many groan year after year
And the crying, the suffering never stops

Vivian Kearney

Moved by a Visit

Just look at how much we have
The impoverished immigrant family
Clapped and laughed appreciatively
Merrily in their almost empty
Shanty flat

And we, the benevolent visitors
Looked around
Trying to find some things
Like enough furniture
To be so glad about…

And cried

Recent Immigrant

You
Look at me
And you see
A foreigner, newly arrived
To a strange land
With exotic
Character, manner, accent

I
Look at you
And search for clues
On how to manage
To acclimatize
Without my far away
Land, circle, friends, culture

Vivian Kearney

After <u>Mother Courage and Her Children</u> by Berthold Brecht

You do what you can to stay alive
Especially for the next generation
The future wants your support
Understand the unavoidable factors

You try as you must to optimize
The brevity of the now and coming day
This is no theater, there are no replays
Walk in my shoes before you criticize

We Are Happy

We are happy
Look at our advertisements
Even for nursing homes
All with ecstatic smiles

We are happy
Listen to those knowing
Sit-coms with laugh tracks
Punctuating every dialogue

We are happy
Expressing ourselves
Through applause, drum rolls
Sending a token few to the top
Of fortune's wheel

We are pursuing
The gods of happiness
Just as our
Declaration of Independence
Bids us

Vivian Kearney

And we're getting close
So very close

We are happy, yes
Or at least dreaming, scrambling
Optimistically

…

Unhappily

That Room

Some people seek fulfillment
    in buying mansions
    a summer lodge in the Rockies
    a winter chalet in Nice

Some people's aspirations
    ascend to penthouses
    in towers scraping the sky
    high over New York City

But our happiness was never greater
    than when we lived in Munich
    by a garret window
    in that tiny little room

– Milo Kearney

Ageism

– How do you dare
To show me what
I'll look like
In fifty-sixty-seventy
Years from now

– Don't worry
Your next co-worker
Will be much younger
With a lot more
Fun energy

– Sorry I forgot about you
Waiting for so long
The youthful waitress said
Rushing by to serve
Her younger customers

– Well, should I try
To go back
To my previous teaching career
Though that needs
More modern skill sets
With my worn out legs,
Lungs, yet?

Prejudice

Man and woman
Boy and girl
Baby
Of color

Dealing with many
Historical injuries
Injustice
Healed not so
Completely

Keep calm
Carry on
On the inclusive road
Of well-being

Together with your neighbors
Of other races and
The white folks around

Not so white either
Also of color
But not of such
A vivid hue

Vivian Kearney

Once an Attitude in School

– Why are you dancing so frenetically
In front of the class I'm subbing
Distracting other students from tasks at hand
Not letting me announce instructions
Spoiling the learning moments
To keep your classmates entertained?

– Because I'm grieving my ancestors' pasts
Conscious of their slavery
Still carrying their chains
On the pain-filled plantation
Of my history

Clouds

That's what
You call it
I wall it
I stall it

Wisps of ADD
Chasing after
Clouds of me

Forgiveness

Under
Every layer of bitterness
Peeled by forgiveness
I find another part
Of my lost self

Beams and Splinters – <u>Matthew</u> 7:3-5; <u>Luke</u> 6:42,43

Understand the one
Whose wounded ego
Bumps into yours
And forgive

Research the fears
That prompt the rebuffs
That worry your heart
And forgive

Be sensitive to sensitivities
Know automatic reactions
And their beginnings
And forgive

Turn your face the other way
For another point of view
You'll see beams and splinters
Hurting you and others
To remove and heal

And forgive

Better Opt for Optimism

Don't go there
In your mind
To lands of dark depression
Avoid paths of pessimism
As much as you can

Where shadowed signs
Are hypocritical
Talks and smiles
Cynical

Instead, ask for
A ticket
To flowered fields
Of optimism
Discussing issues
Hopefully

And half-full glasses
Of refreshing water
Are offered
For the price of grateful
Thanks

Respect Them

Respect the weird other
No weirder than yourself
But in different ways

Vivian Kearney

Dear Sisters of a Certain Age

I know what
Let's all be
Trophy old ladies

Empathy

Faces of people
What do you hide?
Eyes, mine and yours
What do you see?

Look with the eyes of the blind
Hear with ears of the deaf
Sing with the voiceless
To understand their tests

Presently

Presently
At seventy-five
I'm practicing
Some home abilities
I should have honed before
(I can hear my mother sigh)

For example
I've become
A self-styled guru
Of dusting,
Of arranging towels

Folding self
Into smaller spaces

But to whom do I teach
These valuable lessons?

Children, grandchildren
Have far out-skilled
Out-organized, out-learned
And out-taught me

Thanks be to God
Of all mercies

Life's Banners

The banner has gradually become
    almost too heavy to lift.
The headwind blows
    and the fabric shreds.

But it is pleasant just to sit
    amongst the wildflowers
and watch you, grandsons,
    waving your cheerful banners
    higher and higher
    up the mountain path.

– Milo Kearney

In Media

Vivian Kearney

After Cave Paintings

Isn't a painting a needed impression of our world
Translating the boundary-less realities
Into more definitely framed, limited
Two-dimensional colors and forms?

Isn't writing an echo of our thoughts
Codifying our amorphous ideas
Into letters, words, sentences, poems
Creating a permanent record of talk?

Don't dramas, movies, novels, other books
Present relations, possible situations
That segue into highlighted morality plays
Whereby we can find our needed way?

Media Anomie

How should I capture you
Life in all your fluctuations
Thoughts with all your connections
Histories with all your mysteries
Objects in all your presence?

Should I try to portray your essences
With shadings, erasings, paints
Or use the marvelous music of language?

And should I perceive reports,
Clouds and shadows on the window,
Artifacts and happenings as symbols,
Reflections or metaphors?

What is this
Project time meant for?

Classical Radio

Wind leitmotif whistling through our lives
Haunting melodies of Scarborough fairs
Long past. How lovely the memories
Of pale rays through misty gray skies

Violin bees humming through rooms
While clutter buzzes around, refusing to leave
Completely, asking me what the next field
Of projects will be; what flowers when will bloom

Trumpets announcing marching bands passing
How and when will my procrastinating hands
Work productively in structured time
Respecting the clamor of scheduling

Piano black and white keys trip notes in the twilight
Sounding the last hours of the sun's meandering beams
The blues turn royal, cobalt, then into darker purples
Their delicate melodies promising tomorrows bright

NPR – We're All Ears

We sing along and we sigh
We laugh and we worry
We ponder, we smile
We realize, we discuss
What's happening outside

As you draw us into
The global village
We take your talking points
As treasured conversational prizes
Our topical fare to renew

Paris Poet

Dear
Jacques Prévert, dreamer
Singer above the sorrows
That happened to us
During and after
The war

When we,
The thirsty, avid
For new life survivors
Took happy pictures
In the empty streets

Cher
Jacques Prévert, rêveur
Chanteur au delà des malheurs
Qui nous sont arrivés pendant
Et après la guerre

Quand nous
Les rescapés avides
De la nouvelle vie
Avons pris
Des photos heureuses
Dans les rues vides

Comparing Movie Endings

Why do they almost
Always end like that
It seems to be a necessary
Cultural track

An existential need
To have an awed audience
Avidly applaud their approval
As American movies present

Contrast that with the finales
Of French movies not a few
Recommending that at last
We all follow through

With a happy hosted scene
Of a becalmed table, good food
Outside, with family and friends
In a talkative, forgiving mood

To Hold Your Hand

Energized, zenergized, the sixties movie crowd
Relived those songs of transatlantic hope
Remembering the joyous musical talent
The harmony between band mates and audience

Cry, graduates of the sixties culture,
The Beatles won't be playing together any more
Though search and see and understand
It's God as Jesus Who wants to hold your hand

After **Nemesis** by Philip Roth

How does that work, the guilty belief
The forgiveness that is pushed away
The bitterness that keeps digging, digging
The self into a little, resentful place

Rise and shine says all that is beautiful
Good and lovely and try not to cry
Love and be loved for what you were
Now have become and can move towards

Vivian Kearney

After <u>Lord of the Flies</u> by William Golding

The boy with the glow stick is the truth-telling
prophet
The boy with the glasses the eyes of wise coping
The boy with the conch shell announces good
organizing
But the boys with the fire are too careless, letting

The boys with the war paint
The boys with sharpened sticks
Run after, in wild ceremonies, others'
Blood from whatever, whomever

What eventually saved the fictional
Surviving accidental islanders?
…Shocked rescuers from beyond

What will save us from our thirsty
Subconscious crowd drive
Readiness to poison, set fire
To any lonesome garden of Eden?

PTSD – After *Un Taxi Pour Tobrouk*

A French crew with
A German prisoner
In a slaughter-won
Jeep as a taxi
Headed desperately
To Tobrouk
During World War Two

Rattled and blundered
Over the mostly aloof
Yet threatening desert sands

And they almost made it
And almost started looking out
For each other – as brothers
Despite the demands of war

But their tell-tale German car
Wandered once too far
As its occupants now friendly
Forgot that detail
And relaxed too carelessly

And were almost all
Blown up instantly
Across the arid sky

Vivian Kearney

Leaving one survivor
Of the makeshift taxi

Who later cried
When he should have applauded
Military jeeps rolling by
Paraded victoriously
For having killed the enemy

After <u>Eugene Onegin</u> by Alexander Pushkin

A treasure of a country
Girl, Onegin, you threw
Aside, traveling away
To places as cold as your heart

You returned to see your country
Maid turned into a lovely princess
Still sweet, now gracing high society
Enflaming your too late passion

And the banquet musicians played on
And many feasted on your sorrow
Hoping their endless tomorrows
Would be as entertaining

Vivian Kearney

Considering <u>Life of Pi</u> by Yann Martel

Magic the realism
Real the magic
Who is Pi and what is the tiger?

Two dots in the middle
Of vast deeps
Or one?

The tiger could represent
A legend of India
(The universe in his mouth and eyes)
A place that Pi left for good
Feeling sorry they didn't say goodbye

The tiger could even be the young boy
His zookeeper father couldn't quite tame
His worse half, fighting for survival

The tiger may be death
Staring at Pi in the face
Growling its warning
Sharing the same ocean

In the book, the movie
The comfort of Montreal
The farewell to India
Between both places magical realism
Where symbolism touches mystery's veils

After the Movie <u>Trading Places</u>

After all
We all did
For you, so generously
Look at you
With a smart change of clothes
Sporting a different personality

We welcomed you
To our elitist club
Complete with
Sophisticated ladies

But you revolted
Pushed us off
The top of that
Satisfying food chain

Why did you care
That it was
A whimsical, sociological
Experiment?

What did you
Have to lose?

But then after all
Your revolt wasn't
A societal revolution

You found yourself
At the end with your friends
In your own
Exotic playground
Of money

While other
Unhelped homeless ones
Still
Shiver

After the Movie *Canción de Cuna*

Butterflies, bird calls, wings
Of nuns' hats so restricting
Cages, cells, gates, streams
Gardens and flowers inviting

Prayers, dreams, bells, pillars
Fortressing robes, revealed hands
Light often faint, sometimes strong
Grace answering dreams, stories and songs

Discipline, peace, strict religion
Mothering yearning long repressed
Then a gift of love at the gate and
For each nun and the tended orphan
Lives wonderfully fulfilled and blessed

Vivian Kearney

After *Un Coeur Simple* by Gustave Flaubert

A simple maid's heart, clinging, thirsty
For love cruelly denied too many times
Finally released as a flame-colored bird
Into the blue, cool skies above the sad earth

After Finishing <u>War and Peace</u> by Leo Tolstoy

Well, that was my journey with nineteenth
Century Russia in war and peace
(skipped a few pages to the end)

Now to think my own thoughts, praying own prayers
And deal with all the aches and pains
Of aging, as if they were graces
And maybe they are, could be they are

It's as if our younger years were untested
Snow and ice, beautifully sparkling before,
Now melting into water
And soon with the setting sun
Moving into the waiting air

<u>Mona Lisa</u> – Renaissance Muse

Mysteriously poignant the ever unknown
Youthful / old smile that accompanied
The artist from his early fame days
To become his Beatrice with her painted gaze
Leading him beyond his last blurred horizon

In the Internet – The Japanese Art of *Katzumi*

How disappointing – that artifact isn't perfect

No, how interesting the lines, the patches
See how beautiful the golden, broken bowl

Admit it's symbolic of our imperfect natures
Much like our yearning to be completed, useful souls

Vivian Kearney

Shelf Neighbors

Stay
Close to each other
On this bookshelf
Jewish newsletter
And German magazine

Teach each other
Your languages
Paradigms and discoveries

Live and
Let live

NPR Discussion of ***Don Quijote***

A dream within a dream
Is that me, is that you?
An author behind the story's author
The eye beyond the narrator
Questioned existence within infinite mirrors

Some People

Mindfulness Advice

– Be fully aware
Be mindful
Of every part of yourself
Each hour and every day
Zen and mystics say

– No need to persuade us
Certain age people answer
Ruefully, philosophically

Each part of our bodies
Announces – I'm getting older
And need to be taken care of
Minded as much as possible
More and definitely more

I-Worlds

Scary the calm
Frightening the willingness
A whole class in intent
Individual I-worlds
Leaving the real universe
Jumping into the virtuality
Of electronics that might collapse
With one angry flare
Of the sun

Vivian Kearney

Absent From Class

In their talk, ideas, comings and goings
Children are transparent, their thoughts apparent
In spite of teen jargon and attention
To ever-newer technologies

But adult students absent today
How hidden in motive, doings, movings
States and preoccupations, happenings

Who can analyze, guess where they've gone
And when they'll return to participate, to socialize
Under what different health, moods or skies

Particular Conundrums

The spot messing with my garment
That I washed out is now gone
Can't see it. Why not celebrate?
Why do I feel a loss?

The problematic complex now seems dissolved
In another persons's behavior now
Why don't I celebrate the prayer granted
Why look for continued reasons
To mull grumbling thoughts?

Is that my eye's splinter?

Vivian Kearney

Christmas Party Memory

A disheveled vagrant
Drifted into
Our French club Christmas party
As we sang carols
In an old, whitewashed adobe
Art museum

Out of nowhere
Its walls displaying
Oversized impressionistic paintings

Our very enthusiastic, jovial pianist
Pounded the piano and belted out the songs
Encouragingly; she could not
Have been more energetic

However,
As the street person
Helped himself to
Good Christmas food

He shouted vociferously
To the piano player
More pep! More pep!

And wouldn't stop

Convoluted, Memoried, Retrieved

While the party
Grew more merry
In a lonely, dilapidated
Downtown street
Of the border city

Vivian Kearney

Just? Only? Merely?

To say that colors
Are only a play of refraction

To declare that nature
Is just evolving, intertwined life

To pontificate that our thinking
Is merely composed
Of chemical reactions

Is like calling
A woman just a housewife

With a family to help and children to care for
A dwelling to arrange, hands to hold, lessons to tutor
Clothes to wash, rooms to sweep, preparing meals galore
Myriad errands to run, countless memories to store

Let's just say that God, people and creation
Are infinitely more than our categorizations

Parental Prayers

Dear Lord
Don't let it be
That I remark
To our sweet kiddos
I told you so
Why didn't you
My fears mind?

Rather
Let them happily
Let me know
We told you
It would all
Be working out
Just fine

Manic Depression

See and saw
Lack and too much
Serotonin

Lord, give us more
Balance

Whim or Necessity

Really need it or just want it
We ask our eager children
Looking at laughing shelves
Of sugary cereals and snacks
Promising fun and smiles

Necessity or whim I ask
Channeling my adult self
To lament a childlike
Shopaholic addiction
Wandering bright shops
Of clothes a la mode

Maybe we should
Ask what the needs
Are for our spiritual selves
And find the answer hovering above
With God's mysterious, divine love

Vivian Kearney

Visit Again

The grandchildren just left
And the corners of the house
Are sighing, crying

Where are those little boys
Who visited each one of us
Every five minutes
With such eclectic joy?

Once When Subbing I Asked

– Why are you acting this way?

– We can't sew
Though we've been placed
In this sewing class

Why shouldn't we act up
Loudly teasing, punching, distracting
Yelling and shoving
We can't even thread a needle

– Wait a minute
I have at least
That part of
The needed skill set
Down pat
Let me show you

Fast forward
Forty minutes later

– Hey, we've made
These marvelous memorable
Christmas decorations
With our own hands

Vivian Kearney

We're definitely not
Going to leave these projects
In this room
As per your instructions
Or even our teacher's command

We'll bring them home
For our celebrations

And our families
Will be proud of us

This Christmas

Living in the Moment

A little girl, her brother
And their basketball hoop
Just moved away

And suddenly
No sign of those
Other ten, fifteen kids
Bicycling, running, shouting
Playing on lawns, sidewalks
A little dangerously

Did they all leave at once
With that young ringleader
To a never-land
Or a children's crusade
Far away?

And why had we complained
About their idyllic recklessness
Of living in the moment

On our now quieted
Still tree-lined street

Vivian Kearney

Annie and Dora

Two sweet little old ladies
Each shorter than the other
Lived in a run-down house
On a run-down street
In a run-down part
Of our border town

With a big wire cage
In a little kitchen
Holding a stocky, white and gray
Blue-eyed wolf

One sister complained
About the other
Always walking around
In the middle of the night
Because she liked to
Because she had to
Write poems

Some of which
We heard in church

Convoluted, Memoried, Retrieved

I pray that they
Are enjoying
A spacious heaven
With places for
Their friendly wolf
To run and play
Poetically

Vivian Kearney

Karate Novice

The diminutive
Karate girl
Long, curly dark hair
Too tentatively gentle
With her prescribed kicks
For the culminating test
Of a board to be broken

Which was
Patiently held
By an uncritical yet
Determined instructor

The crowd of parents
Held their breath
Hoping along
Sympathetically

Finally she achieved
The needed force
The board and tension broke

And all, relieved
Applauded gladly
Sincerely, without irony

And the now more experienced
Little apprentice
Ran to cry
In her waiting father's arms

Then ran back, resuming discipline
To rejoin the other serious-faced
Initiated stalwarts

Of various heights

Vivian Kearney

What It Takes

To conduct a class
It takes one teacher
And one student

Words to the wise
Motivated ears
Minds and eyes

Thank you, Mrs. Smith

I remember those schoolroom windows
   and the way that they would beckon,
as I gazed out toward the forest,
   and how I would reckon
on escaping again
   during the lunchtime break,
not to return until the next day,
   admonished, but feeling great.

Then in sixth grade came a teacher
   who didn't paddle and didn't shout.
I was moved inside the classroom
   and forbidden to look out.
But, unlike the previous teachers
   I had run from all the time,
she showed me other paths
    than the woodland sort
   by opening the windows of my mind

- Milo Kearney

Vivian Kearney

Beginning of the School Year

Beautiful day
Lily flowers
So many
On the middle school lawn

Maybe one
For each student
Encouraging them
To be brave, calm
Learn to help
And carry on

One Special Day

Today, June 12, 2017
Ben drove at age sixteen
(First grandchild to do so)
From his house way out there
In Boerne's hill country fair
To our house over here
In Northwest San Antonio
A rite of passage to cheer

Vivian Kearney

Lessons at the Hospital

Every moment teaches something
Everyone explains a little more
Measure by measure
Drop by drop
Line by line

As we wander in convoluted woods
Wondering where or what or when
We'll come upon, embark from
The cloudy Jordan shore

Convoluted, Memoried, Retrieved

Why Did She Have to Leave?

Taken from us at ninety-eight
Freda of a thousand kisses
And surprisingly apropos sayings

Memoried, Retrieved

Vivian Kearney

Ever Receding

As if enclosed in liquid amber
Framed by echoing blues
The memories ever receding
Yet exude heart-warmth

Keeping Memories

By the time
I get a blank
Sheet of paper
And write or type

That vague, promising
Idea escapes

Like a bird
That didn't really
Like being captured
Between the bars –
The lines of this page

Even though I promised it
At least
Some longer life
In a garden
Of flowering
Memories

Vivian Kearney

Retiring

Where will we go, what will we do
When we forget what to renew

In the shatterlands of another stage
Pondering shutters of an older age

With Daughter's Help

Today's celebration!
Retrieved the poems
Brought back the collection
From my swirling paper clutter
And teeth of computer objections

Vivian Kearney

With Son's Help

Yesterday computer relaunched
Program reinstalled wondrously
What jubilation!
Our next generations
Continue
To be marvelously adept
With so many needed skill sets

Lifelong Lessons

I can teach you that
I can walk with you there
Those are my interests
Ingrained in my core
I've passed those tests

Others can show you how
To fold clothes, to cook, to garden, to study
Math, music, science, history, technology
To organize a well-run beautiful home
To comment, repartee unerringly

To write, to discuss and explore
Many a peaceful future to balance
And paths of learning to restore

Sail On

Navigating
Differently
At this stage
Of aging

Another sea
Though smaller
Yet with its own countless
Waves and possibilities

Still the moon
And the sun
Here to witness
God's witness
And charity

Grand Central, New York

Why does this feel like home?
Three time visitor
Not a claim
For belonging here
But I do

–Aviva K. Anzak

Together

Look
Through
Your surprised
Child's eyes
O tourist

And tell me
What's right
Amazing and lovely
About my country

So we can sing about it
Applaud it and marvel
Together

Riddle

Sunshine and shadows
Memories and people
People and memories

Which leaves when?

And where do they go
When you can't remember

Vivian Kearney

Gone Too Soon

A sweetness of a nurse
A sympathy of a friend
A wisdom of an acquaintance
A tenacity of war survivors
A staunch secret keeper
A wily argumenter
Many wise family members

A nephew and his father gone too soon
Parents, aunts, uncles and brother
Other near and distant relatives

Death – that poisoned oleander
Took them all away

A charm of a gentleman
An interim pastor
A faraway corresponding uncle
A family mentor, a photographer, friends,
Many well-wishers, advice-givers, teachers

Why did we meet them so vividly
And relate to them securely
No more to meet them mortally

May they be forever blessed and remembered
Let their souls be joyful spiritual survivors

Slippers

Black silk slippers
Can stand on
As if they were
Sole-sized carpets
Can shuffle with
In the early tiled morning
Perfect for the hospital

Decorated with
An embroidered
Red and pink glittery rose
With its baby bud
And bright green leaves

Signalling
There are flowers
Even in the dark

From my dear aunt Mania
Reminding me of her kindnesses
And I do

Vivian Kearney

Once Also Received

Presently threadbare, threadsoft
Once given, once retrieved
From some fifty years ago

Evoking warming and cooling
Souvenirs of a relative
From another country, another time

Grateful for this symbolic
Pillowcase with its pattern
Almost rubbed out, effaced

Gratitude

Remember the people, the love, the family
Who have gladdened
Your life

Know the poetry, the rhymes, the metaphors
The art and music
Of your life

Count the molecules
The atoms, the strands, roads
Through your life

Figure the formulas, the charts
The projects, plans, schedules
For your life

Perceive the opportunities
The miracles, the mentors
In your life

Meet the Lord
Who leads, blesses and comforts from
Above your life

Vivian Kearney

Even More Beyond

Blue as the blue, blue sky
Lovely as the loveliest rainbow
Calming as the most soothing psalm

Many sweet wonders here all around
And even more beyond

By the Waters

By the rivers dark
We wandered
Assimilated
Adapted
In exile

But were still hunted
Haunted by Jerusalem

Yet with our cut hearts
We learned to sing and pray
For all

Including Babylon

Vivian Kearney

Why Don't You Speak, Memory

Malleable
Memory

Manipulated
Created

Distorted
Altered

Constrained
Contaminated

Or stonewalled
True to the grave
Promise of
Not sharing

Retrieved – Three Parables – <u>Luke</u> 15: 3-32

The coin, the sheep, the son
One needed cleaning to be found
The other leaving the rest of the herd
Was rescued with much concern
And the third, the son
Needed patient waiting
And was welcomed joyously
Back home

Vivian Kearney

Triangle of Forgiveness – <u>Luke</u> 15: 11-32

The triangle pattern in the parable
Of the prodigal progeny
Presents father, son, brother
Each having to learn to love
The two twice-saddened others

The father both of his wrong-spirited boys
The envious home dweller the welcomed wanderer
And his own father, so gladly celebrating
While the traveler had to beg his dad's pardon
And embrace his too-distant sibling

There Are Others

There are other
Better inner tapes
Perspectives
Moods

To be had
To be heard
To be retrieved
To be followed

Pray to find them
And lose
The former

Unwritten Diaries

Memories
    unwritten diaries of the mind
    constantly read and reread
    happy pages, calming pages

But, oh those pages
    that refuse to be torn out!

– Milo Kearney

Skies Over Lowlands

Lowlands of sorrow, fearfully anticipating, waiting
For the heavy unremitting hand of depression
Whose approaching footsteps can meld with
The shadow of death, its pitiless companion

But grace carrying angels, like kind clouds
Always hover, saying all is not over, receive
Our gifts of help for the next hour, coming days
From the loving Spirit, both close and sky-far away

Vivian Kearney

Southwest Celebration

Dance hall of Texas
In the northwest part of the city
Star streamers lighting
Our celebrating steps

Dance hall of Texas
In the byways of country
Shining wooden floors inviting
Our feet to party

Dance hall of Texas
Crooning, strumming singers
So we can waltz, two-step
Schottische and boot-scoot joyously

In boots, heels and flats
Black and purple sparkling tops
Long-sleeved checkered shirts
Dark cowboy hats

In bubbles of togetherness
Dancing castles of memories
Stomping, gliding, twinkling
The old sad year away

At a Wedding

Pinpoints of lights festoon outdoor beams
For the festivities, convivial tables, a dance floor
Surrounded by wild pink roses, green grapes
A sweet use of a lovely hill country place

The bride and groom were radiant, joyful
The parents dance-tune thoughtful
Society applauded to move forward
With this milestone of a family's life

Vivian Kearney

Marriage of Personalities

Braiding together once separate strands
Quilting previously embroidered patches

Unweaving confusing patterns
Unpacking wearying luggage

Evolving perspectives collectively
Moving through mindscapes in synchronicity

Eyes wide open to fragilities, abilities
Encouraging interests, goals and ministries

Not only an unpredicted mixture
A miracle, actually

After <u>Thank God for Evolution</u> by Michael Dowd

The triune God
Looking into cave spaces
Searches subconscious corners
With dispensational art

Behold, a dark brook that
Has been watering pre-history
Is kissed by sunshine
As it evolves out

Be joyful and dance
In the cave and outside
For quadripartite-minded man
Is readied to hold His hand

Vivian Kearney

Devotions in Dance and Song

What is our DNA but a coded dance
With its twisting, double-helix choreography
Its parallel bars, like hands, gene points like fingers
Across minuet lines, facing each other

What is our speech but a memoried song
With its inflections, pauses, pitch, sound symbols
All in varied melodic combinations sure
That expand to keep composing a culture

Lord, may our innermost DNA and society's
symphony
Come together to worship, thank and follow Thee

Memoried Our Song

Light as sparkling song
Songs as lasting memories
Sharing, caring voice as love
Here and from skies above

www.ingramcontent.com/pod-product-compliance
Lightning Source LLC
Chambersburg PA
CBHW051756040426
42446CB00007B/389